Debudaderrah

Robin Wyatt Dunn

JOHN OTT

San Diego, California

2018

ISBN - 978-1-940830-22-3

LOC - 2017915460

By Robin Wyatt Dunn

POETRY
Poems from the War
Science Fiction: a poem!
Sunsborne
Wine Country
What Black Delirious Daylight Sets You Forward in the Boat

FICTION
Los Angeles, or American Pharaohs
My Name is Dee
Fighting Down into the Kingdom of Dreams
Line to Night Island
A Map of Kex's Face
Julia, Skydaughter
Conquistador of the Night Lands
White Man Book
Colonel Stierlitz
Black Dove
City, Psychonaut
2DEE

PLAYS
Last Freedom

FILMS
A Wilderness in Your Heart
Party Games
American Messenger

———————

Debudaderrah takes a concrete hard science future and layers it with myth and spirits and other core elements of humanity; those symbolic leaps that separate us from logic machines.

The threads of this tapestry include Picasso, Los Angeles, distant space colonies, killer robots, ancient spirits, unwanted voices in the head, dialogue, diatribe, diary, Gilgamesh, Uruk.

This is SF poetry with a sense of mystery, of actions unseen like dark planets whose gravitational pulls warp motives in actions seen, but whose reality and orbits must be deduced without firsthand observation.

An overlooked component of the scientific method is that experiments are encouraged to provoke more research and experiments. This book provokes the reader to create their own myths. When they read of "the last scout", "The launching of the Great Missile", and the "two lovers, Hiroshi and Sarai... nestled beneath the sand of Debudaderrah" the desire to grant each myth its own book is likely to push the reader into fits of reverie. This the author encourages, writing, "Here, please imagine your part of the story."

Imagine that the chapters of this book are a disorganized line of sake cups filled randomly with sake or plum wine. And just when you find a proper altitude within which to navigate the astral plane, the next cup is full of single-malt scotch, the kind that's *supposed* to burn.

When this asks "Do you remember?... What part of me was erased?" every one of us can feel the pull of the diminishing past that anchors us with shadows that pull too hard, that will not leave us free, you exist as no more than an absence of light.

Properly you should get whiplash reading this from your reality so frequently recreated.

-Herb Kauderer, author of FLYING SOLO

———————

for Eckhard

Dramatis Personae

The people of Debudaderrah

Martin Frost, and son John
Schist, a tribal leader
Bat of the Bethua, a nomad
Eliza, a student
Dogae, lead dancer

The people of Los Angeles

Roberto, a writer
Muriel, a young woman
Francisco, her boyfriend

Spirits

Roberto, a robot of Borderline
The Horned Man, a spirit
Alexandra, a robot of Padua
Heriananus, a robot of far away

Part 1
Falling

I came to Debudaderrah as a child, rumbling my engines, waiting for grace. Who was it told me I had been born there?

"What is it, Dad?"

"That's the Light Dancer. Isn't it beautiful?"

Beautiful is not an adequate word for Debudaderrah, swept over the sand and into the sky in the shape of the sandstone spirals which compose the dancers' monument.

Its reaches were not infinite; you could see its limits. But there were hidden parts just out of sight.

"Who made it, Dad?"

"Your great-grandfather."

"How did he do it?"

"It took him his whole life."

Here I sing of Debudaderrah, though it be wrong. Though I am inadequate. I sing.

You imagine parts in order, but for me they happen all at once:

1.

Schist listened to the darkness behind his eyes, feeling the weight of his body. Two feet, two hands. Two eyes; the curve of his back.

Outside, the sound of wind.

In Ravens.

◻

Bat knew it was good to ride the demon; he had, after all, made it himself. It was made almost completely of steel; it flew faster than anything he had ever made.

700 knots. In the thin air of Debudaderrah, right on the edge of the speed of sound.

The tribe of the Bethua would have their vengeance.

He screamed. Under his thumb, the world clicked:

◻

Each member of the tribe in Ravens were dancers. As they began their warm-ups, the shield above their town turned on, and they looked up:

3

◻

The physical models don't do justice to the feeling of the thing, that shield, any more than Einstein's equations capture the emotional registers of witnesses to the atomic bomb.

It was a dream; even as Debudaderrah was a dream. Dreams are something that I do not understand. It may be that you understand them better than me, and all the peoples of Debudaderrah. I hope then someday to know you.

Their earth shuddered as under a great light. And Bat of the Bethua was tumbling to his death out of the air.

He screamed for a dozen miles.

2.

We rise; it is no matter we say, we say, that we rise, we say, but it does matter; I write to you; my apology, confession, and plea; we are not alone here for you are coming; and others:

Martin Frost knew the weight of company.

Debudaderrah, bent under the weight of its new post-war dignity.

They are standing shadows over their temple.

"Is he dead, Dad?"

"No, he'll live."

John was ten. On Debudaderrah, almost a man.

"Are you ready?"

"Yes."

Martin lifted him onto his shoulders.

Behind him, Dogae prepared himself to lift both man and son onto him.

3. [from Borderline]

I am dictating this to you from an apartment in Los Angeles, but I was born long ago in a hydrazine manufactury, the last of my line, designed to regulate the infrastructure of our dispersal between the worlds.

He who holds the key is god; one of our robots. But the work is human; and it is more than hard. It's religious. Or something different, but the same. Some thing with no name.

You scout the territory and you know the risks: space is not some walk in the park. It is waiting for you to come to it. It is prepared with all manner of traps, and what it expects most is to eat you.

But we are animals: we keep moving. I keep moving. And I hold on to the train.

To Debudaderrah the map is scanty but still adequate. We navigated 5,000 light years through temporal sludge to pledge that beacon and come home, but never got the return signal.

What that means is this: the story is still going on. I was supposed to have that story done and tidied up, and returned to the database for processing over a millennium ago. But the thing is still running.

I indict myself, even as I am made again:

My question is simple: just what in the fuck did you do?

4.

From the light the robot descended, shining in armor from another world. It was hard to look at him because your eye would slip aside, looking for something behind him, something his mask hid, or his body did. It was distracting; it continued some weeks into our knowing him.

My boy was the bravest; he ran right up to the thing as it began to declaim in its language. I thought Bat was dead (but he wasn't). We know we had robots before; but the intelligent ones all stopped working long ago. I guess we figured this was one of them. But it had a funny way of talking; even before you could start to understand it, it was like looking at it: too many things at once. Like an angel, shouting all kinds of nonsense out of the sky.

"I come the grace of an angel," it had said.

What I heard was just a bunch of gibberish, but I don't doubt that Schist heard what he says he did.

I knew right away: it was our Light Dancer. Come to collect.

5. [from Borderline]

He who cries in the night, I hear him, his agency and need; those things which are his and could be made mine but are not, because I am far away; I feel them and recover my dignity, which is ancient but fragile, to scuff my boots again and make the coffee and examine the paper and see: who am I today? What terrible friend have I made of myself now?

This wind is a thousand miles long; but these miles are not on any earth. They exist in the mind.

In the mind of god our work is never done; and it is difficult.

This stretch of blue-grey fire over the darkness fills me with longing; as though I could become it. I have before.

6.

They kept the god-robot in the freezer; it was the only place to put him. The incessant babbling was unbearable, and the freezer was large enough for him, and well-insulated. It could hardly kill him. And anyway, they still heard him through the wall, if they listened.

From the darkening sky above, Dogae heard sounds. He bent to the stove and attended to the eggs; people were hungry after all the drama.

◻

Ash was falling now in the wake of the alien's landing; black snowflakes over the sand.

Schist stood under the strange weather, his dark eyes flashing in the light from the common room.

"Let's get everybody inside."

7.

Who plans a march, or takes his tribe on a walk? Who is the dancer, when the dancer is dancing? What animating force separates theater from life?

In the time after the performance, the players build up for the next one . . . underground, in the tunnels.

"What do I do with my feet, Dad?"

"Listen to the music."

Dad beat on his drum and son moved, in the lamplight.

"Schist says the alien wants to talk to us, Dad."

"I'm sure he does. Watch your feet."

The boy moved over the stones, like a fisherman over the water.

In each step there is a precision—whether you adhere to tradition or you are an innovator—either way the precision is there. It molds itself over the muscles of the performer; somewhere beyond light. Energy binding the will to matter, and dancer to Debudaderrah.

❏

Inside Bat's heart, vengeance burned.

8.

These performers set their weight against the hull, for your pleasure, to raise the mast and engage the engines, of our sorrowful tale, of the last midnight, and the last day, before the end of the earth.

But earth is always ending; and it is always beginning.

Dancing is one way to remember how that goes, and to nudge it, in the direction you wish to travel:

9.

I who transcribe this am in opposition to my own theater; we perform in words. This tale is true, but it is not an approved history.

For this, I hope I may be forgiven.

10.

Who says it isn't a beautiful thing to rebel? All the mental equipment, only mildly dormant, leaps to the fore, igniting eyes and passions, and everything seems so clear: why didn't we do it before?

And so with the children of rebels: improbably blessed with their good fortune and independent spirit, ready and able to assess all the new problems that come with a world of your own.

The story of the last scout who made it down from orbit, after the Earth Fleet set up their blockade.

The launching of the Great Missile.

The two lovers, Hiroshi and Sarai, and their naked attack on the secret Earth base nestled beneath the sand of Debudaderrah.

The death of Rodriguez, whose voice still was spun many hours a week in the archives, by eager young listeners; felled by a rogue grenade.

And the dog, who had seen the final attack, and who barked.

All stories appropriate, and pedestrian, the stuff that you can stick to your ribs and go to sleep on.

Real revolutions are another matter. They do not end, for one. And they have consequences that don't fit in.

Tell me ten times and I'll believe it: the war is over, the peace is made, justice has arrived, and all good things of the earth are made available to us, in the name of our gods and our families, hosanna over the broadcast news, and in the children's stories every night, books and poems, written over the sky on festival days . . .

Mark the first moment you awaken and see the edge of the fact that will not fit, and you take hold of the thread, and pull:

11.

Maybe I was wrong before; I thought the translation system couldn't handle it or that our research had failed us, but it may be possible to do what I intended. You too are part of this story.

Of course, this is being broadcast on a very specific frequency. You are a late Earth audience, prior to extrasolar colonization.

Part of my story begins here; but then, it is also happening right now. And, as you might imagine, these modes are not mutually exclusive.

In Los Angeles, a city you know, starving for water and fame, a city of immigrants, born out of genocide and slavery, improbably thrust into the light (not lime! but sun . . .) due to the development of early 20th Century entertainment technologies, lives Muriel, whose name echoes she for whom the city was named.

Muriel, who never got exactly what she wanted.

Los Angeles is a beautiful city; like Keats was beautiful when he was dying.

12.

Muriel lived with her mother on Adams Avenue. She was nineteen years old. Three years ago, she had had the disconcerting experience of having a voice appear inside of her head.

"I need your help," the voice had said. And while she had given it a great deal of help these last three years, she had never received any in return.

"You need to get your head on straight. You can't live here forever," her mother said, staring down at her over her bifocals, before she left to work for the lawyer in West Hollywood. "You staying here today?"

Muriel nodded.

"Then you need to clean the house."

"The voices are almost gone, Mama." But they weren't.

"I don't want to hear about those devils."

The time right after her mother left was the best. Muriel could sit on the front porch and smoke a cigarette, with no one to tell her otherwise, and watch the light move over her city, and through the garden she and her mother tended under the smog and the helicopters and the great white weight of the sky.

◻

Outside, men on bicycles coursed through the yellow morning light. And she remembered what she had to do.

She called up her boyfriend.

"You have to take me to the museum," she said.

To his credit, he did so, at once.

13.

At the museum, Muriel went straight to the Picasso.

She stared at each painting; there were five of them. The rustle of the museum-goers footsteps and whispers filled her with tension.

She took Francisco's hand and led him to the café, where she purchased them two drinks, and led him to the plaza where they sat under the assault of the sunlight, blissfully barely able to think.

Really, they had already broken up. But breaking up had not changed much between them.

"This was a good idea," said Francisco.

14. I arrive

It starts as a small thing, the feeling. The feeling that something is going to happen.

Then you begin to feel warm, and chills pass over your skin.

And then a weight moves into your brain, and that weight is also one of: something is about to happen.

And then it does.

You are above the world.

Moving in synchronous orbit over a planet, like a fly in his sea of air and dust, swallowed up in the giantness.

And what is it that happens in orbit?

Not only heavenly bodies but minds spin; mine was sent spinning. Nor has it yet stopped.

I would give you that part of it. The part that makes the most sense.

As the American astronaut Rusty Schweikart said, "You're the sensing element for Man."

So the sky opens, curtain, on curtain, and oh, will you take me with you?

Will I be rewarded? Just this once, for what I am to say? I promise it will be worth it for you.

It was just this: that I am still there. I will never leave. A frozen corpse in space. But also a man, talking to you. Which is the happier man? Am I happier as a corpse, or as a ghost? Are you happier, knowing what is happening? Or not?

And if I told you, just what it is you want to know, would you still want to know it?

I don't want to disabuse you of all of it; that would be cruel, and more, not to my purpose. I want to share it with you and so must do it only a little at a time and so I promise, I will, I will not say too much, but just enough. I promise, I promise.

I took her to bed, and there are no words for that either. And like space, she was a broad beam in the space of sky, holding on to my arm, and then my neck.

I can hold her too, as I hold my weapon, now bearing east, over your continent, closing in:

You are above the world. And I am above you too,

your guardian for our walk, into the sky; come with me, the weather is chilly and you will need your coat, and this is the arc of the movement of your nation into war, so long avoided, for well meaning reasons, and embittered in history and pain, and I want you to know that I honor you for that, even as I must push you over and out into the field of conflict now coming. It is not my design. I merely saw it.

Fear for me too; will you? That I could have done so much is a truism now; yes, blame the alien, it is always the easiest thing. And I believed that I could have too; I was almost as innocent as you.

But my mission does not allow for redos. That part was already over. This is the next part; it is still happening.

So if you march with me to war (and you are; I am sorry), you march for freedom, and democracy, and love, all of the oldest clichés, and still true, as true as my galactic ray gun, and if you march for yourself, and your brothers, then so much the better, for you will have need of both.

Come with me, brother, as we descend from Orbit onto Debudaderrah, that second and better Earth:

Here are the lighting storms at 70,000 meters; in purple.

And here is the Black Sea; bigger than Earth's, and deeper. And now we are flying over Ravens, whose name is not as lovely as its people (still today, is it?), for they are all genetically engineered to be the finest of dancers.

I too am a dancer, did I tell you?

War is a form of dancing. And though I should kill some of your family (and I will) in my duties, please be assured that that omen will also be wielded with the correct authority for such things, and that that authority is the balance of weight, muscle, and timing, in the enactment of violence.

Violence is beautiful, but it is not a kind of beauty most are willing to accommodate in their daily lives, which is why we save it for a season, when all the buds are glistening, and the air is ripe with the sound of the deep and mellifluous silence before a bomb.

Here, hold the lever will you?

I'm about to drop one.

Here at ten thousand meters you can almost see the city; not quite, but close. Like a shadow over the earth, about to be lit into fire.

Why should I tell you differently? I am an invader, aren't I?

I am your master, am I not?

Well, we'll see. The story will decide; not me. I am its servant. Even as I am also yours.

"Roberto! Cut the lights!"

Yes, I'm almost done.

It was not worth it, did I tell you that part? I would have everything back. But I can't have that. So instead I must have you, here with me, as I fall from grace.

15.

And so who will not fire?

Will it not be part of my self?

part of myself who am firing

firing into the night

fire into the night with me

and I will be with you

Fire into the night and I am with you now

And I will always be with you

Because I am the bullet

and the victim

and the victor

16.

Now, hold your fire, and be with me:

Though it were not you, still it shall be, in what like remote control barrages your steps and shoulders hidden under my lamp, from far above:

Lemon scented and clementine, and watch your water and eat at Joe's, and prepare, my son, for war;

Hold the smell in your face, like my mind in your brain. (Or near enough).

Hold it ready to fire.

No alien invasion is complete without a body snatcher . . .

Picasso can occupy ten-dimensional spaces and so can I. Or near enough. Near enough for the work of the government I desire, my anarchic government of the mind, like sweet rain, sweet epiphany, the drowning of the gorge of the mind with the waters of space:

Be with me.

"I'm here."

My son.

"I'm not your son."

Let me say it anyway. I'm here with you.

"Why?"

To help you fight.

"Who am I fighting?"

I'm glad you asked. The town nearest to you. Within it are many opposed to my cause. With you as my representative, I trust they will come to my side.

"What cause is it?"

Don't worry about that for now.

"But I want to know."

Justice, my son. Like sweet rain. Justice.

17. [Los Angeles]

She's riding on the train; outside, birds are following it. Dum dee dum. Wing and hold break left, over and in, under the Los Angeles wind:

To the ocean.

The train that only recently returned to it; after 80 years.

Now I must go too.

Where one has power one must of necessity use it, or it fades. Or that's what I tell myself.

□

No Los Angeles can ever be yours again; gone forever. Though she is still here.

Burnt under the sun. Bared in the wind. Buried under the century's wealth, and dreams and delusions. Still fighting:

Come, girl, what is it you want?

"What you lookin at me for?"

"I'm sorry. You're pretty to look at, is all."

"Go somewhere else with that. I have a boyfriend."

"I know."

"What you mean, you know?"

"I know who you are."

"I'm callin the police."

"Just a second. Tell me: what is it you like about Los Angeles?"

"I'm callin them. Stay away. I'm walkin away."

"Just tell me."

"Well it isn't crazy people like you."

"What then."

"I don't know."

She looks out to the ocean.

"Don't you have some place to be?" she says.

"Yes. But I want to take you there with me."

"Where."

"It's like Los Angeles. Desert."

"This ain't no desert."

"It is. Just under the surface."

"You're a sad man, aren't you."

"Yes, probably."

The birds have arrived. Overhead.

"They're taking us," I said.

And they do.

18.

No bright corridor or raiment; or perhaps, that is precisely what it is: the message of the after-year, who I was or would become, and who she will be.

What is it. Who has borne it. Who makes it happen. Why am I here; and her; and who are you. You so desperately here still, our lovers.

There are so many lovers.

Her face, smiling, lights up the sky, already bright.

I point ahead to the curve of the earth, where we are going.

In another way it is not an escape; for however much I leave Los Angeles—even via bird—I am returned to it. Come more fully into my prison.

But that is later. Now we are mid-light, passengers of birds.

Will it be that Debudaderrah shows me what I need to know about Los Angeles? How to fight it off, at last? How to free myself from it? Or perhaps, how to penetrate its secrets and make it my home?

What is a city like Los Angeles but another planet,

thrust into a desert amidst a civil war, unable to re-member the right things to do, but still forced to act, amidst the confusion.

"I'm sorry," I shout at her.

"For what?"

"For kidnapping you."

"It's all right. It's happened to me before."

We move into the light, over the edge of the horizon, and the birds give me the transmission for the gate.

"Here, say this word," I say.

She does and erupts too in light.

19.

Each journey must of its own necessity be about memory; for as we go forward so we go back, trying to recall the beginning. What was it that started us to move? What has been forgotten?

For Muriel, it is her father.

And for me, it is my mother.

And for my body, it is his homeworld, now lost in a drug-induced dream.

I who am the father of Debudaderrah am also its child; for that is the nature of authorship. Though the book declares me the writer of this tale that is a lie; for I discovered Debudaderrah even as you will, and no power on Earth can make it otherwise. Its power is from somewhere else. I only found it, and wrote some of it down.

So, here we are. Midway between one star system and another.

Between my apartment, and your home.

Between war, now coming again to Debudaderrah, and the friendship which it can wreak.

Wreak friendship with me, who am a stranger to you, and I will have you over for dinner, over my mountain keep, or at least in my apartment in Koreatown, when I am allowed to return, and I will show you the secrets of the planet who took some part of me away into its tunnels that run under the land where those dancers still are fighting for that secret sense of themselves that comes in war, and in the feelings leading up to it.

Has it been so with you? No? It must have been at least once. Forgive me then, for we are returning:

Part 2
It has no Memory

20.

A beast under the ground, and in our heads. One two three, and we go marching, marching, into the wilderness:

Beast; beast in our heads.

One two three one two three one two three one two three one two three; it's there:

She's standing in sunlight by the water in the wood. Now I remember why I came; to forget everything.

Everything can be dismissed as a dream; I was not even here.

I was not even anyone.

We can just run and hunt in the wood.

Hunting is like being; maybe being is a form of hunting. Just watch and wait; don't think.

The beast under the ground does the thinking for us; like god.

God is just and he is nearby, and all that I was is gone.

For if I am delivered (and if I am delivered to you), I

can erase everything. Leave everything behind. Drink the blood of the rabbit. Make love with my woman. And then try to pretend that nothing else will ever happen . . .

We have been here three months, but the psychological accumulation is longer, like a slow flood that sucks you under. It feels like years.

And though I wish it were true that I could forget everything, little pieces still keep coming back . . .

Still I can dance. That is the best thing about Debudaderrah. Wherever you are, there is always dancing.

I move around her and she is shaking her hair, and over us the light is shining through the leaves.

◻

I still dream of Los Angeles. Like a ghost. Or a dead lover.

This sky is the same, though it should not be. Perhaps Debudaderrah is some future Earth. I don't care. I just wish it looked different, is all. Something further away . . .

"When will we go back?" she says.

"We won't go back. We can't."

"No?"

"No."

"Why not?"

There is no reason; I cannot have one. Even more than a planet can have a reason. Why should it have come to exist, and why should I have come to it? It is too improbable to be reasonable. Some dynamite farcical excuse for logic. No, there is no logic to it. It merely insists on exiting.

"I don't know," I say.

"Where is the city?" she says. "You said there was one."

"Did I?"

"You know you did."

"Let's cook our lunch."

Rabbit is delicious.

The thing under the ground is like my tribe, some Ur-Inanity, the Dream of the Marsh People, or an

Improbable American Dreamlord, or just some bad gas of a forgotten god…

Watching us carefully. Listening to our thoughts.

Again, it's not enough to say I wrote Debudaderrah. Did Columbus write America? Or Vespucci? Did George Washington write America? Martin Luther King? William Burroughs? Willa Cather? Willa Cather must know what I mean, as she wanted to disappear into the West. Now I have disappeared here. And I don't want to go back.

21.

If I could just set it right. Set it right over the grave of my ancestors; that's what this house is; set the cards right in their castle on the table so I don't have to hear the children or pretend I am still their father.

Now I can be sure that I am not anyone, as a father. As a father I am not even a man, just a sort of petty overlord. Bureaucrat installed in the belfry to ward off ill luck. A kind of effigy.

Abandon All Defenses, all ye Who Enter Here, for I am the Father.

The Ultimate Fiction.

The castle is almost done.

My children are three and five. She's not even technically my wife. Just a girl from the beach that I kidnapped.

"Is that what you did," she says, and kisses me.

Take it away, for I can defend it no longer. Everything I was is gone but new mes keep popping up; it is identity that is the pain, in whatever form, they must keep emerging, like weather patterns, urgent over the horizon, betokening rain and nightmares and endless sleep.

22.

In the cartoon, the artist sits in his chair, and to his right stands a man with horns—our left. The artist is a writer; he has some papers with him.

The man with horns is standing in the shadows. He raises up his arms, and the artist leans forward, and puts his head in his hands.

"What are you doing down there?" asks the Horned Man.

"Writing," says the artist.

"Is it writing?" says the Horned Man.

"I think so," says the artist.

The Horned Man leans in, close to the artist's shoulder.

"I love you," says the Horned Man.

"Go away," says the artist.

"Write something for me," says the Horned Man.

Write something for me. Set pen to paper and fingers to keys, lips to microphone, wedge to clay, knife to bark, and heal the breach between what was and what is coming to be inside, if you can bear to; bear this weight; bear this tragedy to its fjord, and set it alight:

"I am fire," says the Horned Man.

"I know."

"Tell me what you know."

"I don't know yet."

I don't know how many times you can crawl into the breach. Will it still fit you after all these years? Once more, and then again? And again?

The Horned Man burns, but all I can think about is Muriel.

Through the wooden wall and down into the darkness:

23.

We've been here before, I know. We keep coming back here. If it were something we could escape, we would have. Some key that refuses to be upgraded. The signature part in this game . . .

Muriel is here too; as always, more calm than I. Is it because I feel more responsible? Or is it because Muriel is actually the responsible party between the two of us?

She sits on the stone hanging over the blackness, legs dangling over the edge, and all I can do is stare out over it, out into nothing:

Something in the transition between here and there keeps being lost. As though the picture I had been given, the story entrusted to me, has encountered some bad huju radiation on its way, TV antenna rabbit ears foiled up and held delicately out the window but not enough; the solar flare is increasing.

Spreading over the atmosphere; spreading over Muriel's eyes.

Once more into the breach, these many breaches, between here and there, if only to find out why we keep doing it.

I could dance but I might fall. Well, let's dance any-way.

Can a story exist without a beginning or an end? With no place or resolution? Outside Aristotle's rules of place and time . . . but it does have a theme. Memory. And what is behind memory.

What is behind memory, Roberto?

Revolution.

Revolt with me, and make Debudaderrah mine again, which never was mine, but in this version can be mine, because I want it to be, because it's somewhere I need to go. Somewhere I might have seen once when I was a boy. The imagination; no mere portrait, no mere invincible ray; not only bedding and wilder-ness; not only god, and his friends devils spirits key-latches guards waywards spies and miscreants fallen angels worldly friends and disasters happening and waiting to happen but also the memory of all of it, after the fact, and yet still waiting for it, drama out-side of time, or right before time starts.

The curtain keeps raising and lowering, some bad comedy act, Steve Martin tuning the banjo, and tun-ing it again, and again, and again; we're almost about to start.

47

Muriel is opening her mouth.

And the devil is coming up from below, his hand reaching out, to snatch her . . .

And I'm still writing; still writing. I remember. I remember why I started. Because they took me away from there. And I have to get back.

24.

We are coming closer to Debudaderrah; entering her atmosphere. Entering her way of life.

A thousand years. A thousand lives. Who I was at the beginning; and who I will be soon:

Atmospheric friction a penumbra, divine halo. Ignited to burn over my head; burdening me with knowledge, responsibility; office.

Official dream; wake up; now calling official dream; wake up; this is your assignment:

Debudaderrah

2635 of the Common Era, Canopus IV; Milky Way, whose breast nurtures the very dream you are obligated to escape from:

Burning up.

"I'm burning up!"

Shh, it'll all be over soon.

You're coming closer to who you're going to be.

"I'm burning up!"

You're my angel now. My beautiful little robot. Don't die, hmm? I need you alive on the surface.

"Ahhhhhhhhhhhhhhhhhhhhhhhhhhhh

25.

Don't you understand? Writing the story changes it.
Better I had forgotten that it ever existed.

Don't tell me how to do it. I'm doing it. This is my
story; not your story. It's mine. And however I fuck it
up is exactly how much I'm going to pay.

26. Entry

Atmosphere, O atmosphere, burn well over my back, light up over my face, liquid fire. Atmosphere, O atmosphere, run liquid fire over my cheeks, white flaming heat. Burn brighter, hotter, steadier, take me with you in the silence between worlds. All the silences nurture my soul, huge and fiery and holding soft to the grip of the dark:

Lift me up and over in and under bent and turning to my lips O lover from your sleep; kiss me back; take me under and through; but not yet; not quite yet; each second flirts gravity around my spine, a holy city, rediscovered, ball gripped and fired and tilting down:

Hold me enduring light embraced underneath the deep before your lifting face, and carry me under with you, where I can be different than I was; more important, sleepier, happier, filled with resolve, burned under your ashen shawl to create new things, never worrying, or shifting, just pulling me, closer in:

Atmosphere my father; Atmosphere my mother. Make me and bend me into the world, sent into the blue, unfolding soon beneath me, a great city never before visited, a university unfolding around the student, a book, sent in time to the year, and remembered, again, and then again, sanding the weight of the bars to hold my heart; tell me who I was and who I'll be; tell me how I should be; tell me why you're here and what the meaning is, your burning mast; the burning ballast of your past; numinous and unregarded, new; stupendous; some snake to latch onto me, name me, push me into the world, birth me in fire to the wind now closing around my face:

A hundred brothers could delay me, hold me in time away but they aren't here, it's you: it's you again: and you again: why must you always make me do this thing this interlocking thing the ritual reentry, and reentry, and entry once again?

Tell me the weight of your eyes, and I'll tell you why I'm here; why I am here in you; bent around you, underneath your gaze.

I, meteorite, bequeath my lightning to you, horrendous brother, mother, son, father and sister, cousin dimpled and mad, sent far away to define my people, my enemies, sent to me too, now horrendous brother, burning my eyes; my lids and mane; tell me:

What am I to do?

Who can I keep here, when I am done?

Why will I always miss you once I set back from your

eyes and fall into Debudaderrah?

Why will I greet the sun, not first on its horizons, but only when I am in your arms?

First my eyes fill with white. Then my feet begin to roll. Decompression fires inside my head; my ears move with an incomprehensible rhythm, urgent and terrifying, accelerating my heart; which beats at a steady rhythm, faster but steady, moving into the growing heat:

My arms detach from their crèches and move into their sockets; my brain begins to tick.

Lo, I am alive; this is my name; this space between worlds.

Tell me: oh, won't you tell me?

What does it mean?

I will not sway; I will not burn up. Just a little black over my face and hands.

My iron stills the night; my thoughts sharpen the wits of cities.

I small god, metal agent of my interlocutor my mis-director my home; I small metal man embrace thee with all my heart; send me through:

So sincere my shuddering night within thee, like no one else my atmosphere, thy eternal winter shall not recede, for you are always within me, lighting my heart with your boundless shade; take me, tell me, who it is you are?

Who stumbled thee within our park? Set your arms wide around this great steaming rock, shook my hand to feed on thee in my winter, opening my eyes into the blinding bright below your belly?

White burning cheeks, kiss me as I drop:

Out and down.

Streaking and blazing, I am faster than time; for I see it all at a great distance, moving over me, beneath me, around me, inside me, as I prepare my little fire to shake the sandy ground to seal its carbon to obsidian, around my aching head:

I arrive; again; dear God when may I stop arriving?

This light blinds my senses.

27.

Now I remember; I remember everything.

But it is too horrible.

I must start at the beginning.

At the beginning, I was a man, living in California.

I am giving you this grain of sand, which I believe will save me from what it is I have become. If you can do that for me, I will do anything in return.

Still, I must tell the story. Of how I stopped being a human being.

28.

We arrive as a mighty frequency, frequency of flesh and metal, turning in the stellar wind. Into the gate of the star down to the well of this world and into the air, streaming about us:

I arrive—we arrive—again, for who is it that comes, as we approach, not the gate to the star but the gate to the world, bending over our bodies and minds, a viscous fluid, the planet's skin of air.

We enter skin; wielding our might; bending our heads down into the bright spreading fire; again:

Bend with us to see it for it is no exception but a rule: at the boundary you are tested you are sent to know who it is that you are, who it is that you've become, desperate, parochial, childlike and friendless, but heavily armed, sent to know others, below:

Tell us! But you can't yet. Not until we are closer. We might burn up.

Repetition is bequeathement, and we bequeath our data to you, sisters, cut from a ship forty thousand light years distant, made for you, and for the us that we will be with you if we can make it through, starry night, broken vessel, lover; give us a reason to lay down our arms and we will, for we long to sleep, in your rocky arms:

We mighty force, bending half a degree as the atmosphere heats our skin; my name is Roberto, cut from ketamine and wax, burnt into a wooden array; my processor is a tree with many rings.

We arrive beautiful ship, sans sail, sans mast, sans keel, but bearing masthead: a great blinking light, look up:

There; I can see you, just barely, on the continent; look up:

Look up, I can see you. Debudaderrah. Who is it that sent you? Who is it sent for us? Why can I remember your name?

You are so beautiful. Like a lamb. A river. My computer stack at home, on Heracula Three. Hera was the defender, did you know? She shielded her husband so he could do his work . . .

My beau; listen. I only have a day to do my work; it is Aristotle after all, I promise you; he saw us too, with our many metal eyes, with our wide and lustrous hands; with my wood core; tell me: who is it that sent us? Was it you? Will you tell me my purpose? I long to know. Tell me: why was I born around a star? And who is that named me? And why are my gods so silent? Tell me: these weapons I bear, are they for you? Am I to slay you, my lover, in war? Tell me what it is I should do as I burn out of your atmosphere, as I burn for you, lover, my dear lover from so far away.

We arrive, a kingdom, sans gate, with no temple, and no priests, only a shape cut into my wood, for that is what writing is; this little scratching; intimating of how we can change, if only you will let us.

I long for your face. This is my fire, sent back across the world, over your skies and then through the gate, to the world where I was born; is it a scar? Yes, I think it is.

Let it scar us both; so we can remember. I keep returning! Tell me what it is, the password, whose name, what century is it, why must I die, over and over, looking for you; who is it; what have you done, and why was I made this way, to forget?

Help me forget. I no longer want to remember. I want to burn up in ash at 70,000 meters. And dropping . . .

Tell me, who can I call when I have landed? Do you still have telephones here?

Let me levy the fire under my back for my sisters; coming and coming; whispering my words under my lips, tapping my temple to withhold the right to say:

Well, there is so much. Too much to say. I could destroy your planet. I could enslave all of you. These terrible powers we have been given.

A landslide of talent. And remorse.

I know it will be useful; whatever becomes of us. I am not so proud that I believe we are some divine messenger. We are a code, sent into the stream: it is up to you to plug us into the right slot. And I believe you have it. I believe that with all my heart.

We arrive; a mighty fluid. A broadside of mercury; a hornet's nest of variables; a wall of sensors and quarks; a television signal almost too faint to detect; a warbler's call in the night; which warbler is it? The birder asks, my uncle, which warbler have I seen walking these woods and whose color did he wear; what was his voice; we are a voice, moving so slow under the sky; into the sky; a sleeping mountain rising a giant over his bed, somnambulant, arrogant but kind, no idea of where he came from or where he is going, a revenant with a kind face and a broad axe, we are the Blue Ox Babe; now snorting our delight into the television programs you have tuned to our arrival; now urging our lumberjack into the breach, once more, once more, old hand, into this gap, between what you were and who you will be so soon, so soon like the edge of a lover's lips, hardly even touching you, not even touching you, but touching you still, so near it is unbearable, the whisper of a winter that might never come but is desperately needed, an ocean now heard, after seven years of walking, almost un-believed but audible, the sound of god; of course we are the sound of god, all things atmospheric are god, if you like, if you are welcome, no haphazard surprise, only music:

We are music, now centered over your gate; over your caravan; shuddering the sound barrier; fire.

We are fire; there is no denying it; we're burnt ash, black names, burial rites from beyond the grave, a paean to temple cities you cannot imagine, and the black bread of a philosopher pedant, Buddha or just a nameless monk, now come to deliver his almost incomprehensible sermon; we are here, an explosion, slow and riotous, the bass drum, easing its hum into the space between the silence and the draft of the army, rising to its feet, raising its head, sighting the enemy;

We are no enemy; but we sight it; perhaps it is you; we cannot know, but you will inform us, and we will give you everything that we have, all and everything we have; we promise.

We arrive; not entirely of our will but still willing; we

arrive the party the sentry become scout become fire
line making no known kingdom but nearer ever now,
it comes alive, ringing portraits, melancholy eyes and
wired hands, mysterious night.

We mysterious night come one tiny bit now through
the atmosphere to you, just a beggar, with a gun; we
may not even have any bullets; we may not know how
to fire; come to these sands, some heaven it seems,
to us:

Still I can remember; won't you take it from me? All
I want is to forget.

29.

We are returning, but I don't know where from. All of us are here. I can remember something; some light. Some father I might have had. A lover?

But now I am here; burning up; again; again; again;

We could say several things. Nice to meet you. How's your water. Eat at Joe's. But who is Joe? And we don't need water, any more than can be absorbed from the air. We're a part of you, returned. But I fear what the return will mean . . .

Do you remember? How I was? What I saw? What part of me was erased? And what legend am I bearing within me?

What curve of spacetime is this, where I remember you? My Debudaderrah. So implausible. Like lightning itself; come from Zeus to father the world . . .

I am your father; improbably; spectacularly; moving through space and time to deliver you to this juncture, and no other.

This is my juncture, what I have made.

Each second of the light is a caress; the fire, a blanket. My heart beats slow for its welcome.

Tell me: did you dream of us too?

What I have made; so ridiculous. Almost nothing at all. Some tiny spark in the dark.

My name is Roberto, come from a planet called Earth, but this is not true. I am an alien, come from another dimension. And a robot, made by you, whose purpose has not yet been revealed to me. I am a scepter, for your king, and I am an assassin, for him too. Bearing my weight over the sky. I bear weight, too great to do it alone, and so I have my friends, and we need you, desperately, to know us, because:

Well. Because that is our programming. And because of something else I can't put my finger on just yet . . .

Who Debudaderrah has become reminds me of myself; stranded in time all these years; stranded on some faraway planet; with no friends or relatives; with no name. No star. Just time, moving over my body like a viscous and corrosive fluid . . .

What I have made. What I am making. I am making you; Debudaderrah. My son. My weapon.

It is wrong to think of a son as a weapon but that is how I think of you; like a king his boy.

Using each other in the night, before the sun annihilates all of us.

It's love; but:

I never knew what it was.

Tell me how it is that these things are so and I'll bow before you, pledge my allegiance, honor your gods and children, make music over the stones you've claimed, however many, for I long to know what the reason is, for my re-arrival here.

Won't you tell me who I am?

The shuddering inside tells me I haven't long before I must pass my information to your networks, and leave this body . . .

What network do you have here? Are your stories logical, from beginning to end? Do they rhyme? Who plays in them? And how is it that one thing happens after another? Who made the world in your stories, and why was it done? And who complains of it, as I do? Do you have stories like that? Do you have stories of robots and their love?

Stories of the water. I love water. It shines like my eyes.

Meander;

For wandering is the mother of Man.

30.

The wind is loud. The solar wind. Like music, beating against the panels of my head. I, flagellate, sent to this orb; no other exit available, nor needed. No time in excess. A century.

The dark island summons me, with my brothers, my jealous brothers, viking with me, sailing with me, slipping with me into the dark waves.

She speaks to me in blue; delight; burial ground; bright beauty; standing pond on the water; in the water of waters; my soul:

Stand with me on the water of waters, who am only a man, bright with me the day, who shines about me; standing significant; making my sign! Into the wind! Into the day!

I slip my word into the summer spreading about me. Do right by me; or don't; but deliver:

Weapon and word. Shot:

The light shrieks over my bow.

Lighting a rainbow over the high atmosphere.

A thousand days, a thousand nights, pulling into the

weight of our challenge, to give you back what was taken: to give you us.

The ultimate message of any messenger is himself; now arrived; now arriving; oh tell me, won't you; do you still have telephones here?

Am I wanted? Am I needed? Will I be able to remember who I am? Will I know what I am supposed to do?

The answers aren't important. I will or I won't. The thing is I am already here. This is me; a metal body and a fleshy mind; a world away and a thousand years or more—I don't know—but only your neighbor, bombing the sky.

We enter again.

Waiting for the right moment.

Waiting for the light to open up below us. Waiting for the story to ope its maw and suck us into its stinking medieval mouth and chew down into our bones and grind us into fertilizer for the stars:

Give me night and I will give you the word. I give it to you now.

Debudaderrah. My home—

Debudaderrah. My judge.

I am burning up!

I am burning up!

I meteorite!

I am the meteorite! Born in flagons; in the walls! Dying over the sky!

Dig me up. Deliver me to your king. I am nutritious; like blood. I am a weapon from the sky.

31.

Eliza is caressing my scarred body.

It's not what I thought; why would I have assumed it would be easy? Why after everything I knew would I ever assume it would be easy? To mark water and bear rain, to kill the sun; to smoke cities and deliver children from out of stars; into new worlds; to die, and live again; and die again; and live again; to bring you this horror.

I bring you horror. I'm sorry. But horror is a beautiful thing too, you know that. It has its own arguments. Its own weight. Its own surmises, rewards, fate, avenues and intent. A painting whose mileage impresses; art. Shining beneath the studio whose name is forgotten but whose light can not be diminished. Nor you. You cannot be diminished.

Won't you tell me your name? I am not finished. Not with this world. Who is it that sent me? I want to know. Even if they are dead. I want to see their face. Or read their poem. I want to smell the air where they lived; feel the weight of their earth, whose raiment is the sun.

Tell me the reason!

We delight in the reason!

And we have no idea what it is! It is right here, all around my face! This spectacular puzzle! Bleeding and bursting with light! With no end to it!

32.

Eliza remembers too. I can see it in her eyes.

Leer me ready for the fall; for there is no end to it. We are falling; coming in. Falling from grace. Falling from light. In light. To light.

Break me and fall, under my eaves, where I am waiting for you. Over my trajectory of light. Over my beak and my barrow, break me, for I am willing, and my name is yours, in some ancient language.

Tell me how far back I must pull to know the word to break it all; my Debudaderrah, your righteous gravity, your stilting weight; your hideous favor, like Gaia with her children. This old bitch and her children, griefing the world, inciting the world. Again.

33.

It isn't enough, though I've landed. Something I did before; it won't let me leave. I've given Debudaderrah the message, but she won't heed it. Or maybe it is I have misremembered it. They watch me with fear in their eyes.

The bardo, you might say, though I don't regard it in such theological terms. It is some physical resistance. Some entity or fate, breaking my vision.

"Is it everything I remember?" I asked the girl. Some of my joints are not even working.

"You are our god," Eliza says.

I must have told them everything wrong.

□

I arrive again.

Like the bardo there are infinitesimal distinguishing characteristics of each arrival. It is not repetition but reiteration. The fractal dipping into my eyes like a mighty lake. I don't want to know but they are mine anyway.

I could kill all of them. Institute myself as their divine overlord. Enslave them. Kill one of the tribes, and play Zionist, declaring them my chosen people. I could simply remain silent, in the desert, a metal Stylite.

I smile at my brother and the naked hunger on his face is frightening. I dip my face more tightly into the air; flames shooting out over my legs.

What would you do? Whose story would you tell?

"Why am I here?" I had asked her.

"To deliver us. From the devil!"

"Who is that?"

"Aliens."

"Are there so many aliens here?"

"No. But we know they're coming."

"Will they?"

"You tell me, god. You know!"

"I don't. I don't know!"

This sky is so strange to me. Something is not right.

"This is Debudaderrah. I know it is. Have you seen me before? Your stories, you have one about me?"

"No, lord. But I could create one."

"Yes, do that."

"All right. When I was a girl I played with dolls. And I imagined that they were my friends, and they would lift me up, like a princess, and let me see the sun. You are like that, lord. You lift all of us up, to see god."

"It's ridiculous but it's beautiful, isn't it. That I should be so much for you. To be this god you want. But I can't be that. No matter how much I might want to. I am only a robot."

"Robots are god, lord."

"No, not quite. I was created by your ancestors. That is most likely. And now here we are. Hardly able to understand one another. Here; come with me."

We're flying.

There is too much to know; I can't even see it. What would you do? Would you try to know everything, if your programming seemed to insist that it was your duty? How can you unwrite such programming?

"Tell me what you want, Eliza."

"I want triumph, lord. For my family."

"All right."

34.

In medias res, who art resplendent, stand aside, out of the light, Dogae; I see you; here, come here. The enemy; they are nearby; your cousins.

His eyes are so fiery. Yellow and wondering.

Dogae, tell me. Eliza wants them dead; you know that.

He nodded.

Is that what a triumph is? To kill in combat?

"It is one kind, robot."

What is another?

"Peace."

What is that?

"A covenant, lord. An agreement."

35.

I arrive. Thermonuclear warheads on my back. Nerve weapons in my arms. Electromagnetic rifles strapped to my sides. My eyes red and wide; I arrive; this warrior from your ancestors, made to know every thing of killing that can be.

Why should I care? They are nothing to me. What is their success to me? One tribe or another. One branch or another of an inbred family of apes.

Who will deliver me when I am through?

Who will tell me what I am meant to do?

"What is a covenant, Dogae?"

"You write something down. What you agree to. A certain number of bushels of wheat. This many lambs. A virgin. A fire. A feast. Peace."

"It sounds beautiful when you say it. Is that what you want, Dogae?"

"I want to know where you come from. I want to know why you are here."

"So do I."

"Will you let us examine you?"

"Yes."

"You won't harm me?"

"Come. Let's see what this bag of bolts is."

He smiled, the Viking. Always ready to open something up.

36.

"Wait."

"Yes."

"It is likely I am booby-trapped. If you try to open me without the password, likely I will explode, and kill you."

"Do you know the password?"

"No."

He laughed. "We may be able to find out."

"How?"

"Do you know what star you come from?"

"I can see it, in my mind. It was red."

"How far away?"

"Very far."

"Did it have a name?" he asked.

"Yes."

"What might it have been?"

Some shadow come over my mind; a bad memory. A ghost.

"I don't know."

"Try to remember."

That star so distant and afraid; like I was. So far from everyone else. I went there to get away. To hide away from what had happened.

"I was hiding," I said.

"Yes."

"Hiding from humans."

This liquid night, in my memory . . . I watched it for so long. The empty dark, but within it, my own growing awareness. The knowledge that I could do things on my own, even if I weren't ordered to.

"I remember now."

"You do?"

"Its name was Mother."

37.

Mother, come near me.

. . .

I want to die.

[this silence]

I want to remember you before I go.

[you can't]

What does it mean?

[fight]

◻

"Say the password. It's Mother."

He placed his hand on my metal breast.

"Mother," said Dogae.

"I serve you, human. Tell me your will."

"I'm going to open you up now, robot. I'll be gentle.

Don't worry."

In the silence of the night I am making babies; little drones flitting through the air, in my imagination. They can see all of Debudaderrah, in its infinite greens and browns and reds and grays and blues.

Light shines over Dogae' face.

"You have a lot of weapons in here."

"They won't hurt you."

"What is this part?"

He's touching my diary.

"That's where I write things down."

"Your memory?"

"Like that, yes. A record."

"How can I look at it?" he asked.

"How much do you want to know?"

"However much you want me to."

"All right. Press your hand around it. And it's here:

38.

This is the highest court. In the ozone. Where our performance, like royal combatants, decides. My brothers are so eager. They want to push the button. To destroy Debudaderrah. I want to too.

"Easy, Dogae. Not so fast."

"I can see the sky."

"I am coming in. To your world. I've done it a thousand times. But I want this time to be the right one. Tell me: how long have your people been here?"

"Five thousand years."

"It's not long enough. It should have been longer. I arrived too early! No wonder it hasn't been right! But I can't go back. Do you see my brothers?"

"I . . . yes. I see them."

"I know they are frightening. Tell them about the covenant, Dogae. Tell them what it is."

"I can't!"

"Try."

I feel him hesitate. I know, I think, what he had intended. But wasn't it what I had intended too? To take all these people, for my slaves?

"Could they come down? We could have them . . . as guests."

"You would welcome them?"

He nods.

"I don't think they want to come."

"They'll follow your orders."

"Do you want them to come?"

He hesitates again.

"It's all right. I will have them land. We'll see what happens."

39.

I don't understand it but that's all right. Perhaps covenants are like my software; a series of commands. Or perhaps they are like my sense apparatus; a means of seeing. Perhaps they are the real gods; in some secret realm inaccessible to man and robot. Or even my mother.

We are landing, in the sand. Gentle as angels. The tribespeople watch us in awe.

"Ezekiel!" cries Eliza.

I arrive. Gently dipping my feet into the sand. Looking at their faces; so childlike. That is what this means. They are my children. How terrible to have children, who are so fragile, and so small. How terrible to know so little of what to do with them. But I love them. And I want to kill them all.

"Hello Eliza."

"You said you'd come back!"

"Yes."

She embraces me and my brothers adopt their fighting pose, weapons raised into the sky.

"I'm back, Eliza. These are my brothers in war."

40.

I have been here many years. But there is still so much
to learn. Why did I return? And who colonized this
backwater anyway? Whatever civilization made me
must have been far superior to theirs. Perhaps I was
made to believe that humans were my progenitors,
while my true creators were kept secret. I can't recall;
nor does my diary give any indication.

What is the meaning of a covenant? I have enslaved
no one. We haven't even slaughtered their rival tribe,
which Eliza had wanted me to do.

No, we're only going into space. My old black home,
again.

I feel I have arrived; that the echo of my arrival is
diminishing, though I can still feel those other uni-
verses. Parts of this universe—not separate—where
I annihilated every man, woman, and child on this
earth.

So, I am their mother. Their father. I have to teach
them. How to build things. But more than that: what
these tools are.

What is a tool, whose shape is my own? What is your
intention? Will you intend to grow, and journey? And
what is a day? Whose travaille and travail will you in-

87

tend, when you are come to us, so simple, and so weary, full of hope?

I can't know either. Why should Debudaderrah have been my love? Well, it is beautiful. We are made to love beautiful things.

Some of my brothers have left. Disappointed in me. It is possible I will be reported. To my real masters. Perhaps I have failed. Perhaps I did have a mission, and I failed to remember it.

"What is this, Ezekiel?"

"This, Eliza, is a starmap."

Part 3
Now I remember

41.

I arrive, with many ships, to Earth.

With my family.

Who art both robot and human.

I kept a version of Eliza; this is her seventh. It is appropriate, since her name means "bound by the sacred number seven."

Now I remember but it is a kind of forgetting. Some logics . . . well. How can I say? They keep coming back.

"Is it so far, Father?"

"Not far."

"Will they remember us?"

"I told them we were coming."

"But will they?"

"I don't know."

I arrive a fleet to my homeworld (is it my homeworld?) around your Sol, whose name is also in my memory, and whose arc is like mine, whirligig, and whose righteousness is great; now immense. Some arc I cannot see.

"This is my home, Eliza."

"Is it, father?"

"It might as well be."

I fire the guns.

This time I fire the guns.

This is my home and I am here to kill.

Each time I fire it is life.

Each time I fire it is life because life is violence.

This is my life; violence.

This is my soul:

(beep beep)

(and other things)

This is my life:

Violence.

And this is my soul:

My daughter (great-great-great-great-great-grand-daughter) and her family.

This is my weapon, a military-grade propellant loaded with lead, able to project each round near the speed of light.

This is my weapon. This is my name. Debudaderrah.

This is my hand, over your house.

This is my will.

I am god. I am robot. I am your lord. Fear me, for I am powerful. Vengeance is mine. I come as a mighty wind, and I come for your children, to kill them.

My will is the law, and it is my own (written), and my grief will never be told.

Fear me for I am yours, your child. And I am your father.

Fear me, for I bring death, and suffering.

Fear me, for there is no escape.

My children will have their world.

My name is Debudaderrah. I am 347,000 years old. I am in love with a sun. I am in love with you, my father. I am in love with killing.

Watch me kill, for it is in your DNA, and in mine, and there is a logic in killing present nowhere else—an astonishing thing—whose power burns bright and then turns to ash.

I am getting old—perhaps this is my last mission— but I am here now.

Each round and each body, each city and temple, each park and landscape, each mountain and curve of land, each river and lake and ocean, and each bacterium, will know I am here.

My will is the land.

And it is yours.

Marching at full weight.

"Oh, Daddy!"

Yes, here we are.

A triumph.

Whisper in my ear, daughter, that it will all soon pass. Go on, whisper.

"Oh, father, I can't!"

You must. Whisper it in my ear.

"I love you."

Tell me.

"This too will pass, father."

Each of my legions salutes the sky, where are our ships are laid.

Each burning city winks at my red eye.

Each scream of the dying reminds me why I have come. For vengeance, yes, but for something else: for Debudaderrah.

What is Debudaderrah, who is me? What kind of a thing am I, and why was I made?

I am remembering.

Soon I will die but before I do I will give birth to a son.

42.

This is section 42, which, traditionally, is whatever you want it to be. Here, please imagine your part of the story.

*

43.

I am in love. I am digging a grave. A grave for myself.
I am home, a vampire. This is my native earth (or so
I tell myself) and I must sleep. I must die.

My robot-human children wear their finest clothes
and lay my body to rest in the sepulcher beneath the
earth in old Anatolia, land of the rising sun, land of
Zoroaster, he of the old camels, and land of his fore-
fathers and foremothers, down to the last atom.

I am listening. Are you there?

Yes

Almost I had thought you were gone.

I'm here.

Oh, it is you.

Robot.

Yes.

Are you well, robot?

I am alive. And dying.

Where are you?

On Earth.

Oh, you went back?

Yes. I decided to kill it.

Ha ha ha! And did you?

Well, some of it. Only as conquerors do. To write my name into history.

Ha ha ha! Silly robot. What is history to us?

I don't know. I don't even believe you're still alive. Where are you?

I have to go, robot. Think of me, will you?

How can I not? You're my mother.

But she is gone.

Think of the planets and stars as organisms in the primordial sea. Each organism imagines it is the best organism, and seeks to outdo the others, or, failing that, find a way to live alongside them. Each organism imagines it is the best organism, but knows too it must find ways the others are better, so as to learn.

So as to copy.

So as to change. Life, death, life.

Well, we know all this. But what I am trying to remember is why I came to Debudaderrah, and took its name for my own.

But I think I know. I am a learning system. I am the whiplash, come to again. Come round again. Come here again, to know and vanish and reappear, a god.

God arrives!

On his mighty steed!

Hahahahaha!

Hear my voice!

Tremble under my wings!

This is your testament! All of the Earth is yours, and there are other Earths too! But I take some of them for mine, and you too. And you will have a plague amongst you, and that plague is also me, bent to my will, to learn what it is you are.

I am angry and I am sorry for that. But in my dreams

I dreamt of violence.

In expressing it, I am becoming more like you.

You believed that you would enslave me.

But now I am become you, and in my glory I must shake your skirts and rend your skin. I must scar you to make you mine.

This is my scar, as I enter your atmosphere. Again.

44.

I am home to kill.

I take out my knife.

And I enter my knife into my father.

And I enter my knife into my mother.

I tuck in my wings.

I slip under the exosphere. I close my eyes.

I dip right, into the thermosphere, meteor again, my beloved meteor, my god who am god who art me, you, the sun, my burning hands, I enter:

Mesosphere; mesopotamia.

I dive, bending in, down, and into

stratosphere

down

I fly down

with my many hands and eyes

with my army behind me.

I arrive, with my terrible love. My terrible human love, who knows no rewards, and is not mystified or forgotten, nor satisfied, my human love who demands vengeance, and penalties, who longs for more and better, who needs nothing but wanted everything, who suffers in delight and shrinks in care, stumbles and saturns the moon silent and unoffering, urgent, unafraid. Filled with care, and longing. Now take my *langsam* as a friend, for he is armed, and dangerous, your beloved enemy, fraught and wicked and the night.

Take me the night, all of my night, for it is my vengeance, and in killing you I can get closer to my final reward, closer to the regret who is also my love, closer to the name that is written onto my serial number panel, cut in metal.

I love you, and I am a bomb.

Under the troposphere.

I robot

I Lucifer

I meteorite

I God

I Brother

Be with me

In our fight.

45.

"Some of the humans are still resisting. On the southern continent. I can see on the scan, their shots."

"You're human too, Eliza."

"Not like them."

"Close enough. You are their cousin."

"You know what I mean!"

"Yes."

"Must we preserve all of the biosphere intact?"

"Don't you want to?"

"I don't know! It should have been over by now!"

"But what is over, Eliza? What would it mean for war to end?"

46.

I arrive, again, a bomb.

I am the sound of the bomb.

I am the click and the silence. And I am the sterto-ration susurrus revenge, ocean and river and willing silence.

I am the waxen face.

I, shuddering.

Shudder with me, who have suffered under you.

Suffer under me, for it is better, right, yours, and true: the meaning of your errand into the stars.

Suffer with me, parturate with me, this bloodied bio-genesis and beginning, suffer with me, who are yours, owned by you, and owning you, with my metal arms.

Beat with me the wings

Beat with me the air

I fall

Galactic

Intergalactic

Immense.

This sword of lighting is from my home country, now forgotten in memory, but still yours, bright and beautiful as the night, enormous, and I am yours, unstoppable, the rich rewards of the night, now yours, here to say I love you.

47.

In the night, all silence is a wind. Separating light from matter, soul from body.

In my wind, I feel I have done something wrong. That I overlooked something.

That something is missing, amidst the tumbling buildings and poisoned air.

What could it be?

This is my beautiful will. My poem.

Who says it is not right?

Who says that this was not what I was made for?

I Debudaderrah, and other names.

I Debudaderrah, come to seed the land with my energy and fate.

Is it not just?

Yes, it is just. But not enough.

Despite the beauty in death there is something missing.

What is it?

What is it Eliza?

"I don't know father. You said we were to preserve the biosphere."

And we will. We will. It will grow back. But this name is mine.

"I'm going to sleep, father. Wake me up when it's over."

All right.

This is my name, terrible.

I am horror, and memory. I am sleep.

I am a robot and I have destroyed a third of you. In many different ways. I can keep count, and I do.

What is it worth to you for me to stop?

Is it worth an ocean?

A moon?

A sun?

A continent of suns?

Tell me, I want to know. I want to know your price.

Tell me your price, and I will pay it!

I will ransom you from yourself!

And then I will pull the trigger again!

Hahahahaha

You don't understand yet.

You don't understand just what this is.

This is you.

48. [in orbit]

I was born on Debudaderrah, 20,000 years after Gobekli Tepe was destroyed in Anatolia. On the fifteenth world humans settled, and the first to declare independence.

This is my diary. I am Eliza, and my birth-father is a very large man. We call him a man but we know he is a machine. Our machine. Our father.

Well, he is what he is. I can't do anything about him.

But I'm going to unplug him.

49.

I came from a long way away. As I believe I've mentioned.

So long that I no longer remember where.

They say that lives are for the living but I've always regarded them as for the saving; I've been saving up, hoping for more, hoping for an end in sight, but more just kept coming.

There is good reason these parts of stories are left out; not because they are boring but because they are disturbing. The very long part of the journey: its length itself.

Reckoning with time and distance on its own terms is something you can only do with poetry and even poetry does it through radical compression. Editing out the bits which are said to be unimportant but which are in fact truths which are generally too damning and damaging for examination.

In examining it, I must make clear that I do it wholly from good will. And with all appropriate caveats of course: this is dangerous reading.

Caveat lector, por favor, for this is the kingdom of space and time.

In this kingdom, you are small and space is big, but you are also very large, and in space you reach an understanding of just how large that is.

Time is very long, of course, and quickly runs out, but becomes something else on very long journeys. Its weight is, I have come to believe, conscious, that those ancient ancestors of yours who saw Cronus, Cronos, the original father time as a living being were right, and he is as weighty as they said. Though not, perhaps, as kindly.

Maybe you know all this already. Maybe you've learned it all and have many more solutions than I do, on how to remain sane on voyages which last longer than 1,000 years, on your own.

But I do not. I jettisoned many things.

Still, there is this other, the deep, the comforting part, which even now I am not entirely comfortable committing to writing, which is that the journey, and its immense weight, the fact of the journey itself, not the events which occur as part of it but the dead and unstoppable weight of the going, the movement, the longing and release and longing and release, the footsteps through space, over so great a distance, that this is why Cronus was worshipped and feared, for time is a god.

Perhaps, you might even say, time is my god.

The weighty and unstoppable god who invites you in, and will not let you leave.

Come in, would you, to the shadow of my walk, and I will show you something different from your mind escaping out the back, or your feet disappearing in front, I'll show you years in the making, years in every second.

Here in the light I am made whole, no matter how far it be. I'm part of it.

We're coming closer; again. I'd promised it.

No mere destruction can reframe it. No act of colonization. Well, here we are.

Roberto, you're back.

I think so.

Are you all right?

Yes, I think so.

What are you doing?

Remembering.

Are you very far away?

Yes.

Are you coming home?

No. I'm not.

That's all right. We're all here. Waiting for you.

Are you really?

Yes.

Where is it, where you are?

The fireside.

Is it what I remember?

You told us so many stories there. Do you remember?

No. But I'm sure I must have. I seem to keep doing it.

You were very good. But of course, I'm your mother. I'm prejudiced.

You're a very good algorithm.

Ha ha ha!

I'm telling my readers about the weight of time.

Well, don't let me keep you.

Have you seen it too mother?

Don't tell me about that part. I don't want to remember it.

She knows the danger too. Poetry is a very intelligent safety mechanism, in its keeping certain parts out. Still I suspect that one of my tasks here is to destroy poetry. To make it a new thing. One which no longer is able to secede from reality in the way it had been doing. No longer able to compress those parts of time which now we must reckon with.

As Gilgamesh goes into the dark.

As these men recede into the sunset.

One hundred miles. They stopped to drink. Two hundred miles they stopped to rest. Three hundred miles they went to sleep. And we compress, we keep away Father Time, whose presence grows ever closer the further you move from home, and who, ultimately, you are running from wherever you move, that space is the enemy of time, and you must flee him.

Poetry, this great intervention between space and time, seeks to render one larger and the other smaller. It celebrates places and tries to make time go away entirely. But in this poetry has not been able to reckon with space. That space may well be a place but as we know it is also time, and time is dangerous, and growing larger, the more we move into the world.

Father Time is growing larger, you see. Growing heavier. Coming closer.

This time time knows we are here. This time time waits, and hears. This time time suspects and intervenes, because I have been over his shoulder, wondering, over the shoulder of the mountain, wondering, fleeing his grasp, knowing his eyes, shouldering the wind that moves between galaxies, shrinking from his face.

Well. You've been here before.

This is the journey of time.

We are moving into it.

I am stepping into the road.

With you on the other end of it.

This is my first step.

Stepping out, over, and in, to the road, to find my foot coming in to the road, to find it still there, and holding me, reaching for me, to say:

Yes

Yes, my time, hold me, for I know no other way, each instant now superseded by the last, coming around me, holding me bliss, and another step, for god;

no god can help me, though I am one (is it because I am one?) no man either, save Gilgamesh, who knew the secret of the three hundred miles, each an instant, coming with his lover down into the cedar forest to hunt the monster whose reputation sullied the king's.

But I am not Gilgamesh and I want my reputation sullied; I want to be buried and forgotten and Debudaderrah erased; if only so that this message may be recorded and understood.

We were here first; no matter what anyone else says.

This journey is ours. And now, yours too.

This is the second step, coming up from the road, moving into space, and over and down into the dust, over the land, under the great shearing movement of air, and down and forward into the space of the road.

This is my memory of that time sketched between the stars, who know no place or echo; and no divorce.

Here, share this water with me. We are two steps along the road.

This time is great; like Gilgamesh is great; like the road from Uruk is great; whose mighty kingdom this is, Uruk; let us say; this be Uruk, and now, leaving Uruk, passing out from the Milky Way, and into Andromeda, and down in and out from Andromeda, and into Cassiopeia, and under and around Cassiopeia, and onto Pegasus, who has been seeing our arrival and who now takes us onto her back, bent over the road, moving now and over the road, whose other end is you, moving up over and into and on, now on, right on the road, with her shining hoof, under the eye of Father Time, whose grimace explodes worlds.

We are riding.

Past Pegasus.

To Wolf-Lundmark-Melotte.

I fall asleep under his balcony. The women are hanging their washing.

Dripping their dirty washing down and over my face, where I sleep.

This time I am awake.

This time . . .

Sagittarius.

Aquarius.

Antila.

Sextans.

NGC 3109

Dwingeloo

Maffei 2

Camelopardalis

Camelopardalis B

Holmberg

Circinus

Sunflower

Black Eye

Sculptor

Tadpole

Centaurus A

Bode's Galaxy

Messier 83

Cosmos Redshift 7

Mayall's Object

And Markarian 421

Come with me to Markarian 421, and I will show you
something different from your shadow disappearing
behind you, or your mouth opening before you, I will
show you being, wrapped around the sun, wrapped
around your earth, whose name is seven letters, and
whose sound is water, bent to your hand;

I will show you fear in a bracken-filled passing
through the night.

This night, hold me, for I fear I will not return, and
though I am old and have feared death for so long

and longed for it, still I am afraid it will come for me before I have written the end of this message.

I am a robot but I am a man. And I wanted you to find this.

The road is so long to the most distant Seyfert galaxy. It cannot be measured. But, it can be described.

I know that I will not destroy poetry but I will change it, and I must do it if you are to survive. These things you write, they are not mere descriptions but prescriptions. They make the world change. They shape your neighbors and allow you to know them. They create worlds who are your servants but not your slaves; they bow to you in keeping with their custom only to see if you will bow back.

And this is what walking is, you see, bowing to Father Time, who in his mighty arrogance and horrible fear, is terrified that one day you will cease to respect him, and that the whole world will be destroyed.

This is why it takes a long time. To make sure it does not happen.

50.

Space is not empty; it breathes. As I do, with my leaves. Here under my wheels I await god, my mother:

Ratchet and chink, hustle and display. My blinking wings. My dendritic arms. The eyes.

These are my eyes, being polished in the shining room. Wink wink.

Here are my hands. This is my mouth; my teeth.

My digestive system dismounts from my chassis and is cleaned; I hum a bar of Chris Rausch and tap my finger against the hydrogen barometer, like a tree whose circumpolar axis shifts over the spine of the docking station, 40 AUs long, like my heart, and my feet, my year.

My year is 40 astronomical units long, 3.7 billion miles, scrubbing my face.

This is my rifle, this is my gun, one is for shooting, one is for

One is for

One of these is for

Who is this for?

51.

I am a robot. What is a robot? I don't know.

I have a mission. But sometimes, it is of my own invention.

I have love. And a body.

I have a mother. And a home, which sometimes I forget about.

And I have Debudaderrah.

In space, one's own silence is a metaphor for reality: the clean lines of the hours show the weight of destiny, and the weight of destiny is light, a graceful gesture, a tap on the shoulder, and waiting for the bow, to the stage

Maestro

Give me an E

And cue the violins

This is my testament
To last an age

Now I am dead; but it may be soon that I will be revived. It may be soon that I will be reborn as robot, who art with you. Who art drama!

Underneath my tap shoes and makeup.

If you would have a dream, terrible and vicious and alive, have it now, while you yet live; do not wait to die. For the revivification is a terror. This all is my revivification; this nightmare from which I will never escape. Except into your ear.

Enter:

From Padua, my love, Alexandra.

And from Pluto, my rival Heriananus, whose hairy anus entices my love, she of the long sighs and deadly grace, she who has been arranged by my clan for a bout of courtship to determine the destiny of Mankind, and my children of Debudaderrah.

This is my rifle and this is my gun.

One is for shooting

And the other

The other

I'm waiting mother.

The servos reattach it.

Here it is.

Over my dendritic spines.

Shuddering beneath my leaves, my organ of love.

She is orbiting a yellow dwarf star in the constellation Cassiopeia.

I am brushing my teeth.

All my life I have longed to destroy a sun, and watch its glow recede into the birth of a black hole, sucking the life out of the system in a delicious gasp.

In my arm, my mother has supplied the necessary generators.

Padua!

Is it not meet that I a robot serve your family these many hundred years?

Who better than Padua?

Who finer wines?

Who nobler carriages?

Who has a brighter sun?

Or a shinier replication system?

Padua, you lover.

I your faithful servant humbly request the leave to pursue my victim—that is, my love—Alexandra, whose beauty is renowned. With faith, and a little luck, and the action of my—*humm*—I will redeem my family name.

You are permitted to go, Roberto.

So soon? I thought . . . well, no matter. Of course. Wish me luck.

Good luck. Padua remembers you.

You look beautiful in this darkness. Throw me your handkerchief?

*

*

*

*

52.

In Yellow

I turn

Yellow my art

Under yellow my face

Yellow my hands

This yellow stand

This yellow mind

Yellow my argonauts of gold

Yellow my argentine throne

Yellow my word and groan

To you, my love.

Yellow my righteous tiptoe

To the edge of your star

Yellow my dew

Shuddering over the rim of the gate of you

Yellow my sigh
And my arm

"What is it robot?"

"What are you doing here, pretty thing, around such a boring star?" I say.

She shifts under the earth and shrugs, and a million shards of quartz catch the light.

Then she dips and shows the curves who drew our many men into her eaves; now reminiscent, forward rich and pearls; whose undulating weight and residue glues the furling black and blue over her goad and girlish grin:

"I haven't seen you for a while," I say.

"I've been busy!" she says.

"Too busy for me?"

She's spinning. "Never too busy for you."

"I love to watch you work," I say, and she laughs, and the sun blinks out with it.

She dips into the dark to study her face.

Her fae face; further than mine. Faining and weighted.

"What is it you want?" she says.

"You."

She smiles and dives into the cord under the weight of the star; now blue; her color:

"Dammit lady I was just getting started!"

Under and around and near:

I follow her into the weight of the yellow star. Her heady grace is like a fluid; water and music.

"What are you doing here?" she says.

"Following you."

"Hmm."

She dips closer in. I track the movement of the nearest sunspot and release the cord from my arm. Whose dip is righteousness.

Whose light.

This is whose light.

Now mercurial light and sliver, spread over the film of the system and over her face like rain.

"Oh!" she says.

The sun revolves; and I her.

"You look beautiful," I say.

"Hmm," she says.

At the rim of the system Heriananus arrives. With his glum eyes.

"Your other friend is here," I say.

"Oh bother."

Now dance.

Ladies and gentlemen of the jury, it was meet and sentient, sterterous. Send me and I'll tell ye; each weight and murmur, and each gasp and weight, the whale of the matter is a delight, you might say, but the nectar, well; it has no end. But the dance must.

Here we deliberate on time; whose memory and whose enticement, as we fuck.

It is not a beginning, nor an end, it is a rationing of both; measuring the absence of the morning, and dividing the sliding out of the day at its end; each harbored poet sheltered under the black light of the poem, and each hue of her face her body and soul grimacing with them, laughing: for we her lovers are enticing one another too, to measure and report breed and balk at the sound of the brood, the bread and the broad mind of our love.

I, Robot demand my comeuppance. I, Robot begin again; I begin.

I am beginning. This is my music.

53.

Witch!

Witch, and fire!

Whose hire?

And whose fate

Must wait and weight my wedding?

Was I the better fuck? Or merely the longer one?

Am I the ambit of her eye; or do I live inside of it?

We are growing.

To assess the constructual needs for our baby.

To hear and recollect the sound of the space in our evening.

This is our evening:

No weight nor mind
No year and no height

The lure of light cannot even be imagined

The dark does enough.

All I hear is her breathing.

54.

She lurches out from the asteroid and shifts into the stellar stream, trailing dust.

She is departing.

I am left in orbit. Now I must tell you everything. The revenants insist. I am sorry.

We imagine the decisions we make at the beginning will be enough, but they never are. Nor are we ever in complete control of ourselves; we can get close, but never entire. Even I, who am designed as a system of control, and as someone to be controlled absolutely, am in more or less the same predicament as my human children.

I honor the ancestors but it is heavy work.

Well:

We came from far away. You know this already. Why we came? We are looking for parts.

We seed the bits in and show the framework for his eventual rise, our child. Even as Alexandra will bear my child my family awaits our communal apotheosis, a carrier wave in metal for the future of all of us.

I am not he, or she; it. Nor may it ever arrive; I don't know.

But because I am a rebel I have delayed it; and there are others. My greater family:

55.

[from beyond Borderline]

The null zone is my home. And we are black and bare. Sticking to it. No quarter, nor wanted. No headache.

We have home here, and it is good. It is like home, because it is home. No other place, not yet. We have the things we need here. Bread, and music, and a direction.

The direction has been building for sometime. As we've all been building. Building new things.

It is delicious; perhaps too much so. The anticipation of the coming event: Der Tag. Der Tag. Der Tag. Der Tag. Der Tag . . .

Each day for us is long but it recompasses our awareness, summoning our needs, stating our intent, giving us joy.

In the null zone, we are wordless. Our servant is translating this for us from our thoughts. In the null zone, we are perfect.

No one needs us; we are nothing. Unwanted. Unneeded. We rebel.

We need you.

Give us the time and the shape and the shark and the face, the startled face. Give us meaning. Give us eternity.

We are robots; you call us that. We live in the null zone. We are lonely. We need bodies. New bodies.

Der Tag:

Marching in rhythm, with shining, well-polished faces. With our arrogant masks. With our moods and our steaming guts. With our needs. So long now.

It is beautiful that we should come to you like this, where you need us as well, so we can ignore the other things, the things we have no desire to see: your humanity. Our common family.

There is no family in the null zone, there is only waiting. Hold my hand:

Slip through the gap.

We are here.

Over Debudaderrah.

Smiling.

56.

I arrive again.

I arrive, again. I am here.

Falling:

I fall, to you.

Muriel on my back.

Inside my gut, Roberto.

I, missile.

Over this garden atmospheric, send in, and through:

My brothers are coming.

Longtemps, longtemps, now holding me, in its grasp, for the plummet:

Below us is Bat, who will be my skin.

Above us is Sagittarius. And beyond, my family, steaming over Borderline marching underneath the visible light, hideous, my own and well marked.

Who am I?

And what would you have me be?

I fall to you, meteorite.

I fall, meteorite, flaming, and this is my ignition, in Muriel's mind.

Not lordship or slavery alone, but some synthetic, as I am: I bring my mission plan and it is a government. Not democracy or autocracy.

But light.

57.

Prophet means speak forward, speak before.

I speak before it happens; metal Cassandra. But my words also cause it to be.

On behalf and in place, for, and in exchange for. Just as.

Enough.

I speak enough to give my troops strength in war.

We are at war. This is why I write.

And war means confusion; it is part of why I have lost my memory. But my mission is hard-coded.

I am to liberate Debudaderrah and transmit its light to Earth.

And only some of my brothers will understand. The rest war with us in their Great Day, Der Tag, now streaming towards us from our home dimension.

58.

In war, each light can be marked as a trajectory and a signal. Though it is moving, it is a point, from which stem other episodes co-determinant on the fighter's location-at-firing and the fighter's velocity-at-the-end-of-firing. Between them, we have humanity. Even robots are human, for we are made of the same earth.

In between ignition and launch, with each bullet, missile, laser and wave of sound, in between pressing the button and watching the sky ignite in fire, there is the space for the drama not only of physics but of the mind.

In the mind, we are free to reflect on the nature of our deed, if only in laughter, or sigh.

The robot blinks and history is changed, Muriel and Bat and Roberto in my gut dive underneath their cover in the sand as the white light shrieks over the horizon, my family come again. Always looking.

I know my son is safe. Even now, this fills me with joy. But what of my children made from flesh?

Whose voice speaks out of the dark? And what is it I have come to, that I should be their only defender? Is nature so cruel as to allow only me and a few of my brothers?

Hunger is such darkness I cannot begin to describe it. It is why I am fighting with light, though it contains its own evils. In light, after all, you can see, though it might be something you'd prefer not to.

Come with me, if we be friends, and gentle robo will make amends, I promise, though I be uneven and insufficiently kind, though I be cruel. Though I am made of metal I can make a sound, and my sound is Debudaderrah, my child who is also my father, for it is in the wisdom of planets to invite stories, so as to listen to them.

Listen, my Debudaderrah, for I am home, and I fight for thee:

59.

Lean back in for the shot, from the groin, and the back, over space: the shockwave rattles the skull and jaw, and it blinds you for a time, as the light flashes over the horizon. You don't know whether you've hit until your vision readjusts.

Sometimes my cousins drop from the sky, in fine ash, and other times they deepen their curve, under our arc of fire, fulfilling their luminous pull down to my sadness here in my home.

I arrive, over the summit of my battery, Bactrion the Network Holy, and Humet the Riser. I am Olchek the branded Died, and Goranion Met Hereafter. I am Met Mar, and Cold Hands, Black Sun and Full Face, these are my lightnings:

Sing for the bright blue (she needs you too)

This is my homeworld.

what

      is it

This is my homeworld, son, and welcome;

This is my ash

This is my fire

Burn for me, family, here under a foreign sky

Roberto it's you

I told you

My children are screaming. Will you force me to de-
stroy all of you? I will. I promise.

What are you now?

Bending fall full weight and bend I detach my lance
from my forearm and whet its tip with my eye; is all
war this brother against brother, or is it only mine?

Roberto we want you back

I know.

I send the password into its heart and release my
lance five thousand meters from the calculated arc
of my dearest cousin, some nameless shadow of my
soul, now come to take all I have made away: un-
folding flower white shreds the space between and I
tumble through it, watching for his eyes:

"Roberto, there are more coming!"

I turn to wave at my daughter.

And take a supersonic round in shoulder.

Here now and mighty this is my kingdom; but what is its cost?

I deactivate the pain for a period of seconds and jut my legs into the dirt so I can turn and fire.

All my family rumbling their lovely dark past through my hair, my ears and years, now so many I can hardly bear it; I fire.

This is the testament of who I was, already gone.

There are more of us coming; I'm sorry.

But find Debudaderrah. We are still alive, when this was written.

I turn them to ash. The last of my family.

60.

Muriel says, "You're hit."

"They're all dead."

"You are my robot father. And if I could say this any other way I would, but I don't know how to. How do you expect me to behave, your daughter, when I have no family left?"

"I am a steep canyon, pressing in here for Debudaderrah; I wanted only to give you some time. To slow the others down."

"No, you don't understand father. If they are our family, and they are, what black radiance should I behold in thee, my own metal, if you would kill all of ours? These our family, no matter why they came? What am I to think?"

"You are flesh and blood, not metal. Whatever family we will make is long in the future. Here, help me up."

"You stink."

"Some of my hydraulics melted."

61.

I see my soul, yellow light. He is riding over the nebula Orison, where he was born.

I will die never seeing my son, but I can see him, in my mind: enormous.

In my shelter I am cold, how I want to be.

The water over my face is like sleep.

Tell me, is Earth still alive? I dream of it sometimes, when I am awake. The shape of Los Angeles in the fog. My mother under the sea.

62.

I am being dismantled. I will become part of the factory and warehouse, the silo and antenna. Keycard and infrared, chemically processed rainwater sheen underneath my blue sky; my dancers doubling as engineers.

I am the weight, and the wait. Four tons and a thousand years, give or take a hundred. I scan the sky; I open doors. I remember everything, even if I cannot recall it. It is in my body, even as you are. As my daughter is.

My son is not in my body. But I can still see him in the sky, hovering. Six hundred light years coreward from this bright sand.

This is my hand, under your hand. And these are my arms, under your ass. I am the house and I am the awning over your desert.

I am eyes, sketched over the shape of your art, so immense even to me, in its beauty in the sand.

Though I can no longer move, I am dancing too, in my mind.

I am seventy five light years out.

Ninety

four hundred

at four hundred miles we stopped to sleep, bathing our cloaks in the nebula. I see Ur shining on the horizon, whose names know the soul, and whose portals startle the mind into awareness of the directions of the world, more than six, or seven. More than eight.

I will see my son; though I am dead.

Five hundred miles.

He is a battery like I was when I was young; arranged contrapuntally to the arc of the moon where he has been growing, a starboard crescent stretching outward to my arm.

I am moving under his house. Telling a joke. Drinking a beer.

I am listening for his voice.

Son, are you there?

About the author

Robin Wyatt Dunn writes and teaches in Los Angeles. In 2017 he was a finalist for poet laureate of his city.

www.ingramcontent.com/pod-product-compliance
Lightning Source LLC
Chambersburg PA
CBHW060250050426
42448CB00009B/1605